DR EKPO EZECHINYERE

A GUIDE TO CHRISTIAN WRITING

How to become a Christian writer/author

First published by Hebron-Spire EMG 2020

Copyright © 2020 by DR EKPO EZECHINYERE

All rights reserved. No part of this publication may be reproduced, stored or transmitted in any form or by any means, electronic, mechanical, photocopying, recording, scanning, or otherwise without written permission from the publisher. It is illegal to copy this book, post it to a website, or distribute it by any other means without permission.

DR EKPO EZECHINYERE asserts the moral right to be identified as the author of this work.

First edition

This book was professionally typeset on Reedsy.
Find out more at reedsy.com

No vessel braves and conquers the seas without winds.
Lilian, Othniel-Ryan, Zane-Jordan
You fill my sails.
You have my love...

"The world does not need more Christian literature. What it needs is more Christians writing good literature."

— C.S. Lewis

Contents

Foreword ii
Preface iv
Acknowledgement vi
Chapter 1 1
   BEING A CHRISTIAN WRITER (THE ENCOUNTER) 1
Chapter 2 9
   THE POWER OF LETTERS 9
Chapter 3 14
   WHY WRITE? 14
Chapter 4 34
   WHAT DO YOU WRITE ABOUT? 34
Conclusion 44
   Dr Ekpo Ezechinyere. 44
Epilogue 45
Afterword 46
About the Author 47
Also by DR EKPO EZECHINYERE 49

Foreword

When Dr Eze asked me to write the foreword for his book, A Guide to Christian Writing, at first, I was humbled, then I was nervous! But as Eze might tell you, I'll tell my truth.

Part of the goal of a foreword is to tell you what you're likely to get out of reading the book. I will not do that. I won't tell you what you are liable to get out of this; in some ways, that would fly in the face of everything this book is about. Instead, I'll tell you what I got out of it. Because a guide focused on how to be authentic and become a good Christian writer, deserves no less than some genuine reflection and truth-telling.

What I got out of A Guide to Christian Writing was a set of resources. Inside are relevant models that will help me as I continue to reflect on my journey, and how I show up in the world as a minister in the marketplace.

Eze believes irrespective of who you are, what you do, to become a great Christian writer, starts with an encounter! Eze's words, "we MUST know Him intimately. Without intimacy, most things we write will never rise beyond the realm of intellectual discourse". I also got a good helping of anecdotes and stories-some that spoke to me as if I could have been the person writing the words. Others that mirror experiences I've had during my time in business and a few that were new and unique.

Eze provides his point of view- an educated, personal and experienced point of view, but he doesn't force the reader. Rather, he takes us on a journey of discovery and reflections and allows us to decide.

Playful, simple, honest and humble. Gifted and prime. A gladiator of some sort.

A combatant who captivates his readers not with physical swords but with inspired words woven intricately into the fabrics of a story.

Eze's writing style intrigues and lures until you are infused with the theme, thoroughly captivated. This passion of his is enthralling. You start with a story and you end up with an amazing experience!

Then he penned this: "Without an intimate knowledge of God, the Christian writer is dangerous. Such writers could become loose cannons and misrepresent God to and for generations. 'After those lines, I was hooked. It was a blessed assurance of some sort.

Eze's writing style is picturesque. I am not sure there is a formula, but there's a kind of architecture to it. You would like the interplay with words and the style, and lest I forget, he is a comic buff! You will have fun while you are at it.

The path is defined, Jesus the message, Eze the courier, would be Christian writers, the target, and the world, the playing field. It is a guide, a resource, a set of tools. This is the raison d'être of the book, A Guide to Christian Writing. It aims to show the ropes in becoming a great Christian writer that would flood the world with the essence and the fragrance of God.

I believe Dr Eze is worth the read! That's my truth. Now go find yours.

Folake Odediran, General Manager,

General Medicines, Nigeria and Ghana & Country Lead, Nigeria at Sanofi

Preface

A lot goes into the making of a wholesome meal, especially the type that transports to paradise. Cooking is both an art and a science, and the motivation of any cook is to serve up a mouthwatering entrée that gives overwhelming consumer satisfaction.

A restaurateur aspires for even much more. Such would strive to create a cuisine that would give a divine experience, hence, permanently, converting customers over to the restaurant's brand.

We often associate food with ethnicity. Through eating the traditional dishes of some tribes, we journey into their world. For example, spaghetti is synonymous with Italians. In the same vein, the driving force of a Christian writer is to cook up creative and literary Christian meals that will be flavourful enough to convert the world to the Christian brand and reveal the beautiful intricacies of Jesus' culture and kingdom.

It is common knowledge that cookbooks are indispensable for the creation of exotic cuisines. A cookbook shows the key ingredients to use for a particular recipe, the ones to add in dashes and sprinkles, the right temperatures necessary for its perfection, etc.

To the best of my ability, what I have done with A Guide to Christian Writing is to provide a book similar to a cookbook, so that the Christian writer can know the basic things to put together in becoming an outstanding Christian Writer/Author.

My prayer is that by reading this book, you will hear the voice of the Father, discover purpose and take up your pen to become a writing/creative knight in this special division of His Elite army. He needs you, and so does the world.

The sumptuous spread is all yours to feast on. Come, dine and wine. Have a delectable experience.

Bon appétit!

Dr Ekpo Ezechinyere

Acknowledgement

I am a privileged man. Frodo Baggins had his Fellowship of the Ring, and I have my extraordinary brotherhood without whom this quest would never have become a reality.

God, the Giver of inspiration

All my gratitude goes to you.

Reverend Sam Adeyemi

Mentor Extraordinaire, your leadership opened up an artesian well of wisdom and knowledge for me. The spring just never dries up.

Reverend Bode Adegoke

You have an expansive chest I can always rest my head on when the winds of life buffet. It is akin to the stone that Jacob used such a pillow at Bethel. Sir, anytime your heart beats, I hear the voice of God.

Folake Odediran

Ma'am, God created your voice for the world. It booms for the earth to hear. Hence, one can imagine the results of having all that sound energy focused on me. The results are beyond astonishing. Ma'am, you awakened my hibernating form and infused that rare form of energy that only you can inject into sleeping potential.

Blessing Ayemhere

I have bloomed under your headship. Harvard, Cambridge, Oxford and the rest of the best don't have what it takes to teach your rare kind of leadership. Their professors should sit at your feet to learn the arcane secrets of unparalleled leadership that you have perfected into both a science and an art.

Watchforce Exco

It's such a great honour to be part of your extraordinary league of distinguished men and women. Now I know what it feels like to be part of the Avengers.

Throne Worship

Femi Akioye, Ogho Ehilebo, Olayiwola Yusuf, Omolola Amusa, Femi George, Funmi Otusajo, Olamiji Amuni.

For opening my eyes to the depths of God never realized, for the prayers and the prophecies, I can't thank you enough! The heat of your passion and love for God can melt the tundra. Your friendship is a vein of gold and your support stronger than Boaz and Jachin. As much as I love the X-Men, you guys are number one group any day. Exceptional does not begin to describe you, peeps. You are way more. I love una!

Aweni Adams

Your friendship has the stability of a mountain range, a mountain range with a heart. An understatement, still, because words are not enough and will never be. Beside the constancy of your loyal devotion, the Himalayans are chaff-like. Your kind of friendship is one that stays even when a person's shadow deserts. They don't make them like you anymore.

Ngozika Olofin

You are full of more resources than De Beers has diamonds. Before any magician could have uttered Shazam, you brought out the cover of this book like a bunny from a hat! Please lend me your wand. Biko...

Omotola Okunola (Dimpled Rabbi)

What you did was akin to picking a stray to dine at your highly sophisticated table of erudition. From dialogue tags to tenses, you stopped down to groom (teach, mentor and coach). You were the Aristotle to my Alexander the great. If Alexander had you, he would have conquered galaxies and not just kingdoms.

Sholashade Ezeokoli

Graceful coach of nations. The best Sherpa in the world has tons to learn from you.

Okechukwu Okpor

What you do with your camera, the masters did not do with paintbrushes. Thank you for the makeovers.

Bukky Bassey

You gave me the gift of illumination and introduced me to a whole new world. Aladdin didn't do as much with Jasmine. Before you, I was like John Snow; I knew nothing.

Njide Egbuna, Thelma Udemgba Luke Nwoye, Eden. A. Onwuka, Adeyemi Levites, Chidi Miracle, Olubusayo Abegunde, Uche Okey-Onyemobi, Salt Essien-Nelson, Furo-Wari-Tobi, Emilola Shyllon, Chinyelu Oguejiofo, Patricia Ogugua Ajayi, Jolomi Dudu, Chioma Ibeneme Okoye, Onyeka Amukpo, Adeyemi Levites, Chidi Miracle Ejimofor, Aderonke Efunogbon

You armed me with the encouragement I needed to float Christian Writing with Dr Ekpo. This book came out of that enterprise. With friends like you, one can trek the stars. If they had built the Titanic with the support of peeps like you, it would still be afloat. I am grateful.

Tolu Akindolire, Olubunmi Famuyiwa

Thank you for allowing me into the distinguished, starry galaxy that is Creative Minds. With the genius and resources, the group is awash with, a better arsenal for the equipping of writers rarely exists. You rubbed my lamp and out came the genie of penmanship.

Echioma, Nwayineze, Nonso, Chibuzo

What can I say? Without you guys, I would be worse off than Robinson Crusoe, a castaway on a loveless island. I love you. Deeply! I know you know this!

Dad and Mom

Without you, there would be no story. You crystallize the reality of sacrificial love and give it the depths of the Pacific Ocean.

Zane-Jordan

Like Perez, you broke through barriers. You will always be known that, a champion who tames limitations.

Othniel-Ryan

Mighty man of valour, the future awaits your exploits.

Lilian

Your fortitude and support launched this. You are the Apollo 11 to my Neil Armstrong. With your backing, my one small step became a giant leap.

* * *

REVIEWS

The remarkable thing about this book is the effortless way the author made bible lessons relatable to our current age. The author's own story, poignant way of writing, and intended message will appeal to the modern reader, Christian and non-Christian alike.

Other aspects of the book I enjoyed were the ease of reading and continued intermittent doses of powerful lessons, positivity, and 'can do' spirit that emanated throughout the pages of the book.

Unfortunately, this world of inspiration ended too soon, but not before it got me off my seat all equipped to write my truth.

Dr Aweni Adams
MBBS, MSc, PhD, MRCGP, MRACGP

* * *

Many years ago I read a book Life Focus by Jerry Foster that gave me a better definition of life and turned mine around completely.

I have read many such materials and I can point at them at pivotal stages of my life and how impactful they were. Dr Ekpo's book, A GUIDE TO CHRISTIAN WRITING, has joined one of such books.

More than ever before, I am inspired to be a talented writer and influence the Kingdom positively.

Thanks, Doc. You sowed so many seeds here!!! You don't know how much!

Dr. Adeyemi Levites
Senior Vice President, Risk, and Analytics, Reliance Health.

* * *

Have you always aspired to be a Christian writer, but aren't sure where to begin? Do you want to understand which comes first: skill or anointing? Want to know what qualifies a Christian writer?

A GUIDE TO CHRISTIAN WRITING answers these questions and more. In this book, you will learn:

- The basics, fundamentals, and prerequisites of being a Christian writer
- Where to source for inspiration
- Why every Christian should write
- Necessary tools for writing great content
- How to write
- What to write about

Onyeka Amukpo.
Creative Director, NeoVisage Ltd.

Chapter 1

BEING A CHRISTIAN WRITER (THE ENCOUNTER)

Contrary to popular opinion, there was an accountant who knew how to throw a party. He worked with the IRS, but if you wanted a real shindig; he was the go-to-dude.

Though all the trappings of wealth should have made his life honky-dory, his potential was dormant. The bloke was more of a caterpillar than a butterfly. Fortunately, he had a chance meeting with a coach and his life was transformed - the 360° kind.

His relationship with the coach brought out hidden colours and gave him wings. At the end of his life, the accountant, despite his many qualifications, was no longer known for number-crunching but for authoring a timeless bestselling book.

The book of Matthew bridged the chasm of the Old and New Testaments. It is not a surprise that this stunning book is in the vanguard of the New Testament bestselling list. After a hiatus of about four hundred years, Matthew emerges with creative and literary spellbinding fireworks that would have shamed Guy Fawkes'. The man might as well have used a wand instead of a quill.

The research that went into his book was top draw. The tax collector took painstaking raids into the Old Testament and assembled gems which he used to create and decorate a coruscating book. With sublime exquisiteness, the accountant turned scribe aligned Old Testament prophecies with New Testament realities.

The birth of Jesus had made King Herod so antsy that the crazy King put his consultants on the hot seat. In response, they quoted the words of the Prophet Micah. "But thou, Bethlehem Ephratah, though thou be little among the thousands of Judah, yet out of thee shall he come forth unto me that is to be ruler in Israel; whose goings forth have been from of old, from everlasting." (Micah 5:2 KJV).

Here, Matthew showed us experts conversant with texts but divorced from the truth of what they were parroting. They were neck-deep in scrolls but didn't know diddly squat about the deep practicalities of what they taught. Enlightened teachers imprisoned in darkness. Tutors who revelled in facts but blinded to reality. Professors of letters who lacked the spirit of revelation.

It took wise-men from a different time zone to behold the glory of what only existed on the pages of the scrolls of the experts. But I digress.

When the tyrant committed infanticide in his bid to wipe out baby Jesus, the accountant took us down memory lane again to the book of Jeremiah. "A voice is heard in Ramah, mourning and great weeping, Rachel weeping for her children and refusing to be comforted, because they are no more." (Jeremiah 31:15 NIV).

His methodical style of writing was astounding. He held a quill in a hand and a scalpel in the other. The way he detailed the genealogy of the Redeemer was amazing. The job he did in meticulously outlining the genealogy of Jesus, brilliant! No writer of the gospel spoke about the kingdom of God more.

Matthew knew that beyond being a teacher, the Jewish Rabbi was a king whose kingdom ruled over everything, and he captured it all. In proving these facts to the Jews and any who cared to listen, his efforts were high octane.

CHAPTER 1

The whale of work he did must have equated to reams upon reams of scrolls. He must have used up tons of tallow in burning the midnight oil, travelled extensively to interview living relatives coupled with investigative journalism. You just have to doff your heart for this guy!

What about Christmas? We owe enormous chunks of our knowledge about the most glorious holiday to Matthew. For instance, the visit of the wise men and the gifts they presented to the boy-king.

The question is, what turned a finance man into a literary expert, a genealogist, a historian, and a journalist amongst other things? What was his defining factor?\

The answer is not far-fetched. He had an encounter! Matthew met the Saviour. He hobnobbed with The Living Word in the flesh.

Another prominent example is John the Beloved/Revelator? How did an unlearned man get to write five books of the bible, with the last being about the most dramatic literary piece of all time? How did a fisherman put books that grandmasters of erudition cannot unravel till date? His books have the answers to these befuddling questions.

In 1 John 1-3 (KJV), That which was from the beginning, which we have heard, which we have seen with our eyes, which we have looked upon, and our hands have handled, of the Word of life; 2 (For the life was manifested, and we have seen it, and bear witness, and shew unto you that eternal life, which was with the Father, and was manifested unto us;) 3 That which we have seen and heard declare we unto you, that ye also may have fellowship with us: and truly our fellowship is with the Father, and with his Son Jesus Christ.

Still, he dives in still deeper in John 15: 4-5 (KJV): Abide in me, and I in you. As the branch cannot bear fruit of itself, except it abide in the vine; no more can ye, except ye abide in me.

5 I am the vine, ye are the branches: He that abideth in me, and I in him, the same bringeth forth much fruit: for without me ye can do nothing.

Luke the Physician further underscores this with a home run in Acts 4:13 (KJV): Now when they saw the boldness of Peter and John, and perceived that they were unlearned and ignorant men, they marvelled; and they took knowledge of them, that they had been with Jesus.

* * *

Irrespective of who you are, what you do, becoming a great Christian writer starts with an encounter.

If I got a contract to write about a majestic edifice, but my access to the property was only limited to the foyer, at best, my output will be sketchy because the owners did not grant me full freedom to explore the full wonders of the building.

No matter how gloriously I depicted the beauty of that foyer, it would be a drop in the magnificent ocean of the building. I would not have done that project proper justice.

When Aladdin got to the cave of wonders, he didn't stop at the entrance. The riches and the lamp with the genie were deep in the bowels of the cave. To possess them, the lad went deeper and further into the belly of the treasure-filled grotto.

It is the same way with Christian writing. Foremost, you must be born again! That goes without saying. To roar, one must become a lion. Beyond being born again, a vital and deep relationship with God is non-negotiable. Without this, you might as well be an astronaut in space without an oxygen tank.

"O Lamb of God, Sweet Lamb of God" is one of my favourite worship songs. I heard a story about a young singer who sang it at a program. He was so skilful and his voice so mellifluous that by the time he finished, everyone was clapping and hooting. He got a standing ovation for his sterling performance.

Later, an older man did the same number. This time, the congregation was prostrate on the floor, crying. The disparity of the reaction of the same crowd to the same song surprised the young man. Seeking answers, he approached the more mature singer at the end of the program.

CHAPTER 1

"You sang about the lamb, but I know the lamb!" The old man told him.

To write about the Lamb of God and His kingdom, we MUST know Him intimately. Without intimacy, most things we write about will never rise beyond the realm of intellectual discourse.

Without an intimate knowledge of God, the Christian writer could be dangerous. Such writers are at the risk of becoming loose cannons and misrepresenting God to and for generations. Don't venture into Christian writing if intimacy and fellowship (Koinonia) with God are lacking. You might unwittingly become quicksand!

How well can I write about the Great Wall of China, if I have never visualized the length and breadth of it? How would I be able to describe that wonder of the world beautifully if I haven't felt the texture or gazed on the colour of its bricks?

How can I confidently write about the Oval Office, if I have never experienced it in all its presidential dimensions, or with unusual diligence studied the works of the people who have?

I am usually mesmerized by the magic of Hollywood. However, they usually come short of excellence when portraying Nigerian scenes. Many times there is a mixup of accents and cultural distinctiveness. This is because of limited knowledge and many times, nonchalance in carrying out adequate research.

To write the Ten Commandments, Moses spent days with God on Sinai, away from all the hustle and bustle of daily living. Paul wrote many letters in prison when he was in lockdown and insulated from the distractions of everyday happenings. These men wrote completely plugged into heaven's main and fully immersed in the atmosphere of the courts of the King of kings.

God is the electrical source, the Christian creative is merely a conductor. A wire not properly connected to the source cannot conduct properly and at worst can electrocute.

John wrote that Jesus is the vine and we are the branches. For us to bear much fruit (writing and creativity in this case) we must remain in him. A fruitful branch is always and seamlessly attached to the mother tree. To disconnect is to die.

Before John ascended through the portal to heaven to get the injunction to write, he was in the spirit on the Lord's day. The apostle was saturated in a divine environment. But beyond that, he loved Jesus with unusual passion. He was so close to the Word that became flesh.

Christian writers cannot operate on their own, they are conduits, pipelines of divine flow, ladders between heaven and earth. They are God's quills expressing heavenly realities on human hearts.

A Christian writer is an arrow, a weapon of change. An arrow must be able to fit snugly into the fingers and the bow of the archer. There is a kind of attachment, a bond between the projectile and the shooter (Legolas and his bow and arrows come to mind here).

It takes a lot to be a veritable Christian creative. Heaps of hard work, plus a mix of dedication, denial, sacrifice, faith, and patience (sometimes, this element strains one to a breaking point. To wait on Him and in His presence is a must, but not always easy.

To write the law, Moses stayed on a mountain with God for more than a month). There's no denying the place of skills, learning, a vibrant network, great marketing, and so on, but they are just the trimmings of the salad. The main constituent of the meal is fellowship.

Christian art takes more than being adroit. Over the years, I have seen many secular artists become Christians, but only a few maintain the creativity we knew them for and even fewer became brilliant in their new vocation.

Skills alone don't cut it in this kingdom. It's the anointing that makes the difference. As eloquent and erudite as Paul was, he told the Corinthian church that he did not approach them with the enticing words of men's wisdom but in full demonstration of the spirit and power.

Anointing amplifies skill and breaks the yokes of limitation. David couldn't have killed Goliath with only a sling and a stone. Undoubtedly, skill is golden, but it plays second fiddle to inspiration.

CHAPTER 1

In Babylon's best university, Daniel and his friends learnt all the ramifications of the arts and sciences. But what made them superior to their classmates was God's empowerment (Daniel 1:17). That was the differentiating factor.

It is not by power and not by might; it is by the Spirit of God.

"Many times this type might never come without prayer and fasting," said Jesus.

Skill-wise, Nathaniel Bassey is arguably not the best trumpet player in the world, but we cannot deny the anointing and grace at work in his life.

There's always a price to pay for the anointing, though. It doesn't fall like ripe cherries.

We write to minister, inspire, and transform lives, but we are not sufficient of ourselves. Our sufficiency is of God, He is the one who makes us able ministers of His message. It is the grace of God that abounds towards us, that makes us sufficient in all things and fruitful in every good work.

Pharaoh's magicians were skilled in the dark arts and could replicate Moses' phenomenal acts. It initially was a battle of wits and skills, but the power of God gave Moses' rod supernatural advantage, and it swallowed the evil lords'. Skill is exceptional, but power is greater. Small wonder that Moses told God that if He didn't go with them, their exodus would be pointless.

Moses' deep intimacy with God was what brought about the book of Genesis. He travelled down the chute of time and documented stories that happened aeons before his birth. Now, that is serious writing/creativity!

It is noteworthy that secular writers also engage the supernatural. Stephenie Meyer is the author of Twilight, the YA book that made vampires famous in recent history.

According to Wikipedia, she is best known for her vampire romance series Twilight, which has sold over 100 million copies, with translations into 37 different languages. Meyer was the bestselling author of

2008 and 2009 in the U.S., having sold over 29 million books in 2008, and 26.5 million in 2009. Meyer received the 2009 Children's Book of the Year award from the British Book Awards for her Twilight series finale Breaking Dawn. Meyer was ranked No. 49 on Time magazine's list of the "100 Most Influential People in 2008", and was included in the Forbes Celebrity 100 list of the world's most powerful celebrities in 2009, at No. 26. Her annual earnings exceeded $50 million.

With no prior experience as an author, the idea for the Twilight series came to her in a dream. According to Meyer, the idea for Twilight came to her in a dream on June 2, 2003, about a human girl and a vampire who was in love with her but thirsted for her blood. Based on this dream, Meyer wrote the draft of what became chapter 13 of the book. She wrote from chapter 13 to the end of the novel and then backfilled the first 12 chapters. Meyer's work has been criticized for her overly simplistic writing style.

Disparaging comments about the quality of her writing skills have been made, but no one can deny her prodigious results. Simplistic style (as some people put it) or not, no one can deny the power and the impact of her books. This underscores my point. INSPIRATION OVER SKILL.

Though some would think this is pure hokum, a discerning person would know that the brilliance of some books, series, and movies exhibit a touch of the supernatural. It stands to reason because, in our world, the spiritual has ascendency over the physical, and the intangible over the tangible.

The authors of the bible wrote as they were inspired by God (2 Peter 1:21). The Bible says that there's a spirit in man, and the inspiration of the Almighty gives him understanding.

Chapter 2

THE POWER OF LETTERS

Two middle-aged men emerged from a house. One of them, face a mask of rage, banged the door so hard it shuddered.

"Who died and made him Caesar?"

"Julius, calm down. He's only a little boy," the other man responded. His tone was placating as he thumped the back of his older brother.

"That's the point, Erastus. He has suddenly grown wings because they thrust him into a position he should never have smelt. The runt couldn't even look me in the eye as he spoke. Let's get out of here! I need a stiff drink."

Erastus, smiling, drew his brother close in a side hug.

"That is more like it. Julius, the thirsty fish. Let's stop at Valentina's."

"Well, after encountering that upstart, no palliative will appease better than a tankard of wine."

He chuckled. Erastus drew him closer still, and they walked away, laughing.

Inside the room the brothers left, the young pastor held his head on a table that groaned from the weight of scrolls and manuscripts. The leadership crown he wore got heavier by the day, and he didn't think he could carry on.

Rubbing his eyes in weariness, he noticed the scroll his mentor had sent to him that morning. The events of the day had overtaken his excitement and buried it under tons of other debilitating concerns. Feverish with anticipation, he opened it and read.

"Let no man despise thy youth..." The words leapt at him and ignited a fire in his heart.

That night, Timothy, timidity ditched like a worn cloak, preached up a storm.

The congregation had their mouths open as he spoke. After the service, Erastus and Julius approached him sheepishly and apologized. Timothy told them that there was no offence taken.

As they left, he slapped the scroll in his hand, looked up to the roof, and his face broke into a radiant smile. "Thank you, Apostle Paul," he whispered.

* * *

In all the Bible, the story of creation is the most captivating for me. When I read the book of Genesis, pictures usually pop and swirl in my head. It always brings the power of words to the fore.

And God said...

His words set a chain reaction of extraordinary events in motion.

In the beginning, was the spoken word, but the written word brought the spoken word to our consciousness. Without immortalization through documentation, how else could we have known what God said?

Words in all forms are powerful, but without the written words, the spoken word would lose its potency through the thickets of time. Like an aged and overused knife, its edge would become blunted.

If we do not give the spoken word a framework using the skeleton of letters, it becomes wobbly and loses shape. Time dilutes it and some of its original meaning would get lost. In the written form, words bridge time and dispensations without undergoing major shifts or changes compared to when relayed only by word of mouth. Writing provided a body for the spirit of the spoken word.

The King James Version of the Bible has remained the same since 1611. There have been countless spin-off translations, but with the consistency of a mountain range, the original has stood the test of time.

If the bible hadn't been written, it would not be as powerful. The life-transforming words within would have just been floating in the air without lasting substantiality. Penning those words gave the eternal word ubiquity and accessibility.

If Moses hadn't written about the story of creation, there would have been no countering standard against the flood of Darwinism.

Assuming the story of David and Goliath was left only to oral narration, an over-enthusiastic or drunken griot might have put forth that David used a trebuchet to kill Goliath instead of a sling and a stone.

Written words are binding. They underscore the credibility of spoken words. How would we have believed that the ages will end if God had not instructed John amongst other writers to put down his revelations? God specifically told John to write!

After the emergence of COVID-19, in the quest for answers, many Christians got buried neck-deep in the book of Revelation. In the bid of exhuming clues about the present standing of our world, Eschatology became a hot topic. After hundreds of decades, the book is still relevant, extremely so.

A world without written words is rudderless. This was why Moses repeatedly instructed the Jews that escaped from Egypt to write the words of God on almost every available surface so their testimonies could pass down the generations without losing momentum and effectiveness. Written words give a foundation for generations to build their identity.

Written words make truth irrefutably binding, which is why contracts and testaments are undeniably powerful. The Bible is so powerful that, in the Middle Ages, to keep laymen disenfranchised and prevent them from challenging authorities and the status quo, the ruling class denied them access to the book. Unfortunately, this is still some people's reality now.

Written words give direction. Daniel discovered the prophecies of Jeremiah through the documentations of the prophet. That was how he got to know the number of years allotted to Israel in exile. The knowledge he gained inspired him to pray, and the prayers affected world history and dynasties.

Books are powerful. Some have revolutionized the world.

The Origin of Species is in the vanguard of the atheistic movement.

The Communist Manifesto by Karl Marx and Freiderich Engels helped to birth communism.

Mein Kampf by Hitler fueled the uprising of the Nazis that killed 6 million Jews.

Martin Luther King learned non-violent protest principles through Gandhi's writing.

Some of these books did the world more harm than good. But either good or bad, none of these books come close to the Bible, not by planetary miles. We might as well be equating the firepower of an ancient revolver with that of the latest jet fighter. But that still falls short. No comparison would ever suffice. To persist in the venture would be sheer folly.

The Bible is the most powerful book, ever! That it's the greatest best-selling book of all time is no fluke. According to the Guinness Book of Records, as at 1995, about 5 billion copies had been sold and distributed worldwide (Wikipedia).

Unfortunately, with this outstanding book, many Christians are like a Jedi Knight who doesn't know what to do with a light-sabre. Heartrending, I tell you. Study to show yourself approved (2 Timothy 2:15)... Paul strongly admonishes Timothy.

A major factor that helped in the birthing of this book was a cartoon. Writing is the primordial form of cartoons, songs, and movies, amongst other things. When I wanted to start the online coaching course, Christian Writing with Dr Ekpo (https://drekpo.com/courses/basics-of-christian-writing/), doubts assailed my mind like a band of Visigoths attacking a Roman fort.

While feeling that I wasn't ready and didn't have what it took, serendipitously, I came across a cartoon, Spiderman: Into the Spider-Verse. In the animation, the protagonist, a boy named Miles, felt he wasn't good enough to become amazing like his hero, Spiderman. Spidey told Miles he would never be ready and to take a leap of faith. I leapt with the boy and here we are. This book blossomed out of the seed of that course.

Writing is a powerful tool for transformation. Anytime you write, you have the potential to change the world, especially if the Bible is your greatest source of inspiration.

Chapter 3

WHY WRITE?

WE WRITE TO SAVE THE WORLD BY INTRODUCING THEM TO THE LOVE OF GOD

Jesse could not believe it. This could not be happening! No... Evie was broken-hearted. He had caught her red-handed, and there was no way she could explain the incriminating graphic pictures that flooded her phone away.

"I am sorry, Jess. I don't know what came over me. It was the devil."

Distraught and overcome with regret, she knelt before him, unconsciously wringing her hands. Tears streamed from her eyes into her mouth as anguish choked her vocal cords. Tasting salt, she croaked, "Forgive me, please."

Jesse couldn't bear to look at her. Running his hands through his head, he paced the room. With the ferocity of a feral beast, the claws of betrayal tore through his heart and slashed his soul to tiny ribbons. The agony was too much to bear. It surrounded him like an unrelenting fog.

"How could you do this after all I had done for you, Evie? How?!" He

CHAPTER 3

hissed. Flames of hurt burned in the pits of his eyes.

Recently, they had flown her brother to India because of a life-threatening condition. The treatment had run into millions of Naira, but Jesse had gallantly borne all the bills as if it was the most natural thing in the world to do.

Her father was a palm wine tapper and couldn't foot the bills, but it was no big deal. He had never seen more perfection in a human and had loved none more. Every time his heart pumped, Evie's essence flooded his vessels to every part of his being.

He had also paid her tuition at the best online business school in the world. Her face-to-face sessions had made travelling necessary, and that was how she met the serpent that stirred up the trouble in their paradise. She had fallen cheaply and resoundingly from the revered perch of his heart.

Jesse couldn't bear it anymore. Anger thrashed like a restrained wild animal within his being. He clenched his fists in his pockets to prevent himself from resorting to anything stupid. If he lashed out, it would be disastrous, so he kept his wrath tightly reined in.

Finally, he reached a consensus. She must leave. He would banish her from his life forever. The only way he could deal with the treachery was to delete everything about her from his memory banks. He would collect his keys so she couldn't visit anymore and change his locks. It was also time to get those mastiffs he had been wanting to buy.

"Get out Evie!" Voice still barely above a whisper, he pointed to the door. "Get out!"

"Please, Jesse! Please!" She pleaded, tears flowing like the Euphrates. What they had was more precious than Havilah's gold, but her self-destructive nature had corrupted everything.

"Out!" This time, he forcefully opened the door.

When she saw the wrath in his eyes, she scrambled up to her feet, took a last look at him and the posh room before stumbling out of the house.

He was about to close the door when his eyes locked onto something in the distance, and he froze. "EVIE! WAIT!"

He started running as she turned. The hope that flared in her eyes was quickly doused by bemusement. When he got to her and pushed with all his might, Evie shouted in alarm and hurt. As the force threw her off into a bed of flowers, a tank filled with water fell on him.

Heavy rain accompanied by fierce winds had fallen the night before, and the forceful gusts had shifted the water tank above the house. The plumbing company called in to fix it was working when a restraint broke off.

Jesse, about to close the door, saw the tank swaying. In a shot, he figured out what was going to happen.

Water was everywhere as Evie, dazed, walked in a haze of horror to where his body lay, soaked and broken up. "Jess... Jesse..."

Her unfaithfulness had led to his death; he had given his life for her. Tentatively, she touched his unresponsive body, then screamed and screamed and screamed...

* * *

The world is a Pandora's Box chock full of pain, selfishness, heartbreaks and direly needs healing. Fortunately, love is the panacea for humanity's problems. But human love will never suffice because, by default, man is self-centred.

Man's only hope of survival is the divine love of God. The earth cannot do without this. We can only find the redemption of our planet in Christ's unconditional and selfless love. He emptied his blood, gave His life to save the world.

Love stories seldom go wrong. The story of the world and God is one of love. The best romantic tale ever! Adam broke God's heart through the greatest act of betrayal, but God's love never gives up on humanity. God's love is fierce, and He loves ferociously!

This is timeless. No romantic story beats it. Not Romeo and Juliet.

None!

Using writing as an artistic tool, we can capture and convey His love for the world in different ways. We can also use all kinds of allegories to convey this message. The most important thing is that as a drowning man needs oxygen, the world needs the love of God. And God will never relent in His love despite the unequalled treachery of man, never!

WE WRITE TO GIVE INFORMATION AND INSPIRE TRANSFORMATION

In Christian writing, information and transformation go together like conjoined twins; hence, the Christian writer must always strive to go beyond the dispensing of ordinary information.

If Peter Parker had not become the amazing Spider-Man after the radioactive spider bit him, the bite would have been inconsequential. If a doctor administers drugs which didn't give any curative value to an ill patient, what good is that consultation?

Remember what Jesus said about tasteless salt? The value of salt is in its potency. The worth of Christian writing is in its power to transform. Jesus' words come to mind here, "It is the spirit that quickeneth; the flesh profiteth nothing: the words I speak unto you, they are spirit, and they are life." John 6:63 KJV.

There must always be jewels of revelations within the information we purvey. Revelation kindles transformation. Without the power of radioactivity, the spider that bit Peter Parker would have just been another irritating arachnid. It was the radioactive power it possessed that triggered the monumental metamorphosis that turned the timid nerd into a superhero.

Therefore, a Christian writer must always write under divine inspiration. Remember again, "for the prophecy came not in old time by the will of man: but holy men of God spake as they were moved by the

Holy Ghost." 2 Peter 1:21 KJV.

Jesus said, you will know the truth and the truth will set you free. When we present the truth in a way people cannot refute or refuse, we ignite transformation.

David said that he gained more wisdom than his teachers and elders through the word of God.

A scroll found after decades led to a spiritual revolution in Israel during Josiah's time. The possibilities are endless.

WE WRITE TO UPHOLD KINGDOM STANDARDS AND VALUES

Some common values thread through the whole of the holy book. One of them is hard work and diligence. At the beginning of time, the first time we saw God, He was working and worked so hard that despite His divinity, He had to rest after his endeavours.

Hard work defined the patriarchs and the apostles. Jacob was so diligent that he made his employer wealthy.

Joseph's first dream was one of assiduity. The dream was unusual. A splendid dream should be one where one is having a swell time and not stacking stuff on a farm. He was working in a field (I have a book coming up on this soon). Joseph was having a field day working and throughout his life until he ascended the throne and beyond, this precious quality was ever-present.

Moses' industrious culture was so embedded that even as a fugitive, he did not become a layabout. The prince of Egypt became a shepherd. Mind-boggling!

Paul worked so hard that he dared elements, beasts and empires to achieve heavenly objectives. It is no surprise that he "boasted" of working harder than all his contemporaries.

The Kingdom has no room for laggards. The good book commands such people, "Go to the ants..." This is very pertinent for today's

CHAPTER 3

generation where people wander about expecting to hit pay dirt with minimal effort.

Jesus' work ethic was astounding. It will always bode well for us to remember that the full expression and embodiment of God said, "My father worketh and I work!"

Another great kingdom value is adding value and problem-solving. The Bible is a book brimming with problem solvers. David solved a national problem in Goliath, Jacob worked out husbandry difficulties for Laban, Joseph resolved a food problem for the world, Daniel decoded an issue that was giving Nebuchadnezzar ulcers and sleepless nights. The prophets rectified a myriad of conundrums. God anointed Jesus of Nazareth who went about doing good and healing all that were oppressed of the devil (Acts 10:38).

Humility is another Christian trait that is heading the way of the dodo. We have empowered people who because of the designation of their offices or endowments deem themselves more special than others.

The heroes of our faith were very simple people, Jesus inclusive. Peter was aghast at Cornelius' action when the centurion bowed to him. He made the Roman know that God is no respecter of persons and He is also the only One that is worthy of worship.

I dare say that if many people in our day would have patted Cornelius on the head and appreciated him for recognising their greatness and anointing. Fanning out their feathers more than peacocks, they would reckon that they are worthy of such obeisance. For crying out loud, they had hobnobbed with the son of God and Saviour of mankind. To cap it all, Jesus told them He would build the church on the rock of their revelation of Him.

The time has come for us to bring these virtues to the surface again, especially because of the ones coming after us.

WE WRITE TO SHOW THE WORLD THE BEAUTY OF GOD'S DIVERSITY

God is "multi-diverse" and that shows through our diversity since He created us in his image. Your personality and your story differ from mine.

Therefore, when we write, we each reveal unique aspects of God to the world. And one doesn't have to be a particular or special kind of person to write.

You can be an accountant, a scientist, a housewife, anything, or anybody. What makes the bible are the stories of everyday people like us.

Hannah had infertility issues. Thousands of years later, the story still inspires (The revelation of this helped birth my son). You don't know who will get inspired by your story. I have always found the stories of the folks in the Bible invaluable because anytime I find myself in a jam; the Bible is my go-to resource. Through it, I can study the lives of people who went through the same challenges I face and how they handled them. Nothing is new under the sun.

David had a wilderness period and wrote about his experiences. Psalm 23 inspires me no end. I can't get enough of the truth that God provides a table for me in the presence of my enemies.

You can write your travails with God embedded in the centre of it all so that others can have their faith fired up. Our stories are for His glory. Jesus emphasized this when His disciples asked Him about the man blind from birth.

This is what the patriarchs did. They used the loose threads of the issues of their lives to weave mesmerizing tapestries that had an overarching theme of God. Their stories blessed the world and made God famous.

The story of David and Goliath teaches that with God on our side, we can become giant killers. Mind you, the giant doesn't have to be a mountainous, dreadful man. It could be anything that stands as an obstacle before you and your God-given dreams. The Bible amongst other things is a book of allegories.

Our stories are not about us. They are for God and humanity. We are smack dab in the middle of a never-ending story between God and men. On one hand, we show off the might and character of God. On the other, we reach out to bless humanity.

No matter how famous actors are, they are subject to the screenplay. Actors, unless they are also producing the movie, never own a story. The story is usually bigger than the actor and he/she is subject to the studio, the producer and the director. The work of the actor is to fulfil the dream of the studio/producer and to provide a delectable experience for the audience.

For example, the story of the three Hebrew guys revealed that our God never leaves his own helpless, especially when His children go out on a limb for Him. He has such a presence that a fiery furnace turns into an air-conditioned space when He shows up on our behalf. Fire cannot consume itself. Our King is a consuming fire.

That story also encourages us to have faith in God, no matter how fierce our situations. Irrespective of how uncomfortable our trials, with God on our side, we wouldn't become toast. We will come out of infernos redolent of roses instead of smelling like ash.

Stories are beyond the storyteller. Their essence usually breaks through the barriers of time and waft into the future. It is through stories we affect generations unborn.

Abel drives this point home. Though dead, the story of his life still spoke.

YOUR STORY IS UNIQUE!!! YOUR STORY DIFFERENTIATES YOU! YOUR STORY IS YOUR BRAND!

Your story makes you the most special being in the world, the good, bad, and seemingly ugly of it. Our stories are like fingerprints. No one else has yours. Thus, if you don't write your story, a piece of life's jigsaw will be lost.

You would have robbed the world of something profound because no one else can replicate your story. This is even more so when you are God's special courier with a specific message for the world.

God has put an affinity for different things into us. Writers mostly write about what they love and know about, hence they show God off in his multitudinous majesty. When creative Christians gather, they are like the Avengers, X-Men, or Teen Titans.

Each superhero comes with a unique subset of gifts and narratives. The consolidation of these distinctive gifts makes us a powerful and indomitable force.

We also have different personal revelations of God as shown by unique books of the bible. Hosea showed the unrelenting love of God for us, irrespective of how wayward we might be. Lamentations revealed the sorrowful state of affairs that follows egregious disobedience. The books of the Kings underscored the influence of leadership. Songs of Solomon waxed strong about romantic love (Kiss me with the kisses of your mouth, for your love is better than wine. Heady!).

The dimension of God that I know about prosperity might differ absolutely from yours. Jacob saw a vision about genetics and hit a gusher in animal husbandry. Isaac experienced the power of supernatural drought-resistant hybrid seeds. Joseph was a consultant that could make predictions and projections about the world economy. Daniel could unravel complex equations. These guys all struck gold through different dimensions of the many-sided grace and power of God.

It is the original experiences that the patriarchs had about God that brought about His different names. Abraham encountered supernatural provision and called him, Jireh. Moses witnessed His power on a battlefield and gave Him, Nissi. We vicariously view those dimensions of Jehovah through their stories until their realities manifest in our lives too. What if they had hoarded these marvellous testimonies and never wrote? For one, some great songs we love today would never have seen the light of day.

When I write from my perspective and you write from yours, we offer the reader a wholesome and a more comprehensive understanding of The El-Shaddai. The reader sees God from a wider lens and becomes better equipped for life and living. The promises of God make us partakers of his divine nature. We endow others with such possibilities when we write.

The Bible is a study of God's mosaic nature.

The book of Numbers is about accounting, record keeping, and census taking.

Ruth is about commitment.

Leviticus is about the niceties of the law in different spheres of life.

Nehemiah is about real estate, architecture, and town planning.

Kings and Chronicles are historical, political, and governmental.

Lamentations show that God can use anything, even jeremiads, to pass His messages across to humanity.

Paul's letters are full of admonishments, especially the ones to the Corinthians and Galatians.

Judges is about superheroes.

Fantasy and sci-fi movies can emerge from Revelation and Daniel, and so on.

There are no limitations to the genres of Christian writing. You can write about anything and everything. Jael was a housewife, but her story made the pages of the bible. You can be a baker and write about your special cupcakes, but somewhere in between, you chip Jesus in as the bread of life.

Moses was a prince, Paul was a lawyer, David was a shepherd, Solomon was a king, John was a fisherman, Luke was a doctor, Titus was a mentee, and the list goes on. Such sweet miscellany! The variety of subjects and authors in the book of books are beautiful, and that need not change.

Anybody and everybody can write!

My father was a barber and told me years ago that he wanted to write his autobiography. I didn't take him seriously because I wondered who out there would want to read his book since he wasn't a president or some famous bigwig.

However, when he persisted, I gave him the idea to do a voice recording and have it transcribed. The book turned out to be beautiful and is in the pipeline for publishing. While editing it, I got to know and understand him better. It also drew me closer to his experiences. Even if it doesn't become a bestseller, it would surely become a family heirloom. He also infused heavy doses of evangelism into it. He inspired me to no end. If my dad can do it, you can!

TO SHOW THE CONSISTENCY OF GOD THROUGH THE AGES

When the writers of the Bible wrote, I am sure they did not have the foggiest idea that their poems, stories, and "mere" letters would outlast dispensations.

Now, through their writings, we can see God through the ages, especially in the areas of context and culture.

Life is changing faster than the Flash, and it's all we can do to keep up. But God's values never change! In the next few years, the church will no longer be the way we know it. But if someone writes about the present-day church today, a pastor in the next 50 years when his church might completely be online would get to know how churches were being run in the past. He might get a revelation that will propel his ministry forward because nothing is new under the sun, as King Solomon said.

CHAPTER 3

I did some consultancy services plus editing for a writer recently. It is a beautiful book that, amongst other things, shed light on the missionaries that brought the gospel to northern Nigeria, Reading about how they sacrificed life and limb to make sure the gospel reached the ends of the world lit a fire in my heart. Some of them lost their lives and were buried in Nigerian soil. Though I live in a different timeline, their stories motivated me and made me know that there was a quality their faith had that is missing in ours.

They were not softies tossed back and forth by the changing tides of life. They were die-hard veterans of the cross with rock-solid convictions. They inspired me. Such is the power of stories.

The letters that John wrote to the churches are still relevant today. A struggling widow today after 4000 years can read about the widows in the book of kings and get the insight that will transform her life and her family's.

Recently, while reading where Elisha told a Widow to sell and live, I realized that marketing was a huge part of my life that I hadn't been paying attention to (you can read the full story on my blog-site, https://drekpo.com/biblical-truth-on-marketing-and-selling/).

This was the same way New Testament believers consulted with the pages of the Old Testament to unravel and buttress the truths of their day. For instance, Psalm 22 and Isaiah 53 gave deep revelations about the death of The Christ thousands of years before He was born. Stories can be prophetic.

Writing bridges the past, present, and future. To get more clarity about Covid-19, many people had to resort to things recorded about other plagues that took place in the past. The knowledge gave better clarity on how to deal with the present challenges. If someone hadn't written, we would be shooting in the dark without an iota of hope.

The story of how Noah navigated the flood and how Isaac came out on top during a recession are also relevant references.

Our writings convey the immutability of the values of God and the dynamism of his methods of operation.

A Christian scientist can write to show that God is the bedrock of science and technology, etc.

MAXIMIZING OF POTENTIAL

Diligently hitting a gym doesn't leave anyone the same. It is the same thing with writing. When we write, we enlist in an intellectual gym and use all of our intellectual wits and muscles.

In the bid of writing, we do thorough research, spend interminable periods on thinking, meditating, reading the bible and other books, and get the help of mentors for the journey. Studying, learning, and engaging the rules of writing, grammar, and other helpful writing minutiae are as vital as blood for the craft.

Writing changes us in no small measure. It helps to establish one as an authority and turns our Clark Kent into Superman.

Super stuff!

WRITING HELPS THE MENTAL STATE

Writing can be a valve for stress-letting. In a world where stress is taking a toll on the human populace, it induces a sense of calmness. This is the reason some people keep journals and diaries.

Therefore, for people who stress easily, writing can be a survival skill. Writing things down also gives clarity and perspective to situations that had hitherto been difficult to get an insight into.

CHAPTER 3

WE WRITE TO BATTLE SOCIETAL ILLS

We can also use our stories to deal with prevailing ills in our societies. Growing up, fables about the tortoise and the hare were used to reinforce morals, and those stories stuck with us. They taught us not to lie, cheat, etc.

Rape is evil, and the horror of it is unmentionable. We can educate and raise awareness against such malignant tendencies using stories in the bible. Amnon, the first son of David, lost the throne and his life tragically because of rape. The consequences he incurred over a few minutes of passion were too dire.

Shechem, an ancient city, was plundered because its prince raped Dinah, the daughter of Jacob. Her brothers avenged her violation and in a blind rage laid waste to the city and killed all the men.

In a world where many women get the short end of the stick, we can help to change the landscape by writing about heroines like Esther, Jael, Rahab, Deborah, the daughters of Zelophehad (Mahlah, Noah, Hoglah, Milcah and Tirzah), Mary, etc. These ladies and many more made history and are outstanding models for our daughters to emulate. Let's bring the stories of these heroine's to the fore.

WE WRITE TO GIVE HOPE

It is heartbreaking that scarcely a day passes these days without a case of suicide hitting the news. Being bereft of hope is a dominant cause of suicide. Many cannot see beyond the blinds of the present into the brightness of a glorious tomorrow. They cannot visualize any ray of light at the end of the tunnel of ongoing challenges. It's tragic.

The bible is full of stories of men and women who went through fiery trials, but gritting their teeth, they endured until things changed for the better. Joseph, Naomi, Ruth, David are notable examples amongst many others.

The bible rightly captured it when it said, weeping endures for a night, but joy comes in the morning.

The temptation sometimes is to use a scene to interpret a whole movie. What if Joseph had given up on his situation in the prison and thrown in the towel or given in to a more dastardly act?

What if Sarah and Hannah had used their temporary situations to define the rest of their lives and have drunk deadly substances to bring their pain to an end? There would have been no Isaac or Samuel.

Hold on. You will yet laugh and all you are going through now will become like a bad dream. After Samuel, Hannah had more children. Peninnah who tormented her with the pitchfork of mockery is a bygone name while Hannah will forever be a mainstay of our faith.

Imagine how much we would miss if we walked away in the middle of some of the greatest movies ever made because things became very unpalatable in the middle. We would never get to experience the full richness of those classics. The beauty of a movie is getting immersed in it to the end and also enjoying the trajectory as it unfolds.

Picture me buying tickets, popcorns, and drinks to watch Lords of the Ring or Star Wars. Imagine me getting so distressed when the Balrog makes Gandalf fall into the dark hole or Darth Vader gains an upper hand that I leave the theatre.

If you knew the stories and that Gandalf would come back stronger and Luke Skywalker would emerge victorious over Darth Vader, you would find my tantrums, waste of time and resources ridiculous.

I am a scriptwriter and the best movies are the ones loaded with insurmountable conflicts and tension. From the stories in the Bible, we can show people that they can't rudely interrupt the stories of their lives because of some unpleasant scenes (This does not negate medical care and counselling). What you are going through now is part of your hero's journey that will give you the golden yarn to craft a bestseller or blockbuster tomorrow.

I know it's not as easy as it sounds, but winners are those who see things through to the end. Jesus went through a gruelling time and at the end proclaimed, "It is finished!"

He called us to walk in His steps. Stubborn faith is a necessary weapon every Christian must possess. With the shield of faith, we can withstand the unrelenting barrage of the enemy.

Many stories in the Bible show that the end of a thing is usually better than the beginning thereof. The story of the redemption of man for one. The story of David and the Amalekites is another excellent example. The situation made a mess of his leadership credentials. What if he had thrown in the towel when the Amalekites carried away everything that mattered to him and his guys wanted to stone him to death? Instead, he encouraged himself in the Lord and saw the situation as a temporary setback. Ultimately, he recovered all and even much more.

Let's use our stories to convey hope in all its sunny essence. Beyond the stories, let's also reach out to people with copious amounts of love. Love is healing...

WE WRITE TO INSPIRE

With COVID, church congregations have been on lockdown. But that shouldn't grind the wheels of the church to a halt. The early church flew on the wings of letters. Paul was many times on lockdown, but detractors could not stop his letters from circulating. The letters ended up reaching places he could never have reached by himself (indeed, all things work out for the good of the Christian even when we can't see or know it. This story is also similar to the Romans leaving John to die on Patmos without realizing they were enabling him to open up the most powerful chapter of his life).

Those letters fertilized the soul of the fledgeling church and still inspire the present-day church today. This is the time for church leaders to write more than ever before. We should also use this instrument post-COVID. It is not a surprise that one of the greatest strategies of marketing in our internet age is email marketing.

TO DISCREDIT THE WORLD AND ACCREDIT THE WORD

The world's way of doing things is most times opposed to that of Christ. Many Christians bemoan the fact that our children are continuously exposed to poisonous materials injurious to the soul, especially through the media. The big question is, what alternatives are we bringing to the table? Life abhors a vacuum.

"If you don't like someone's story, write your own." — Chinua Achebe.

Every song, movie, book, creative work that lays a siege against the Christian faith started with writing. No matter how mighty a studio is, it can never produce a movie unless there's a script.

This is where you and I come in. There's a resurgence in the following of many things that represent Baal in our present world. The Christian belief system is being subtly diluted under an insidious attack.

That didn't just happen. Crafty machinery plant suggestions and innuendos that take root in the soul like weeds and slowly suffocate Christian values. Seeds of suggestions if not strongly countered get engrafted and become life-draining oaks, especially in these times that many people are becoming "woke" and turning their backs on Yahweh and His ways.

Unfortunately, we are mostly a throwback of Emperor Nero who was monkeying around with a fiddle while Rome burnt.

There's a highly acclaimed and well-written book that caused a lot of ripples. It was beautifully written but glamorized ancient idols. On the surface, it would seem like another literary book, but it was full of hints that could derail Christians with fragile faith.

I read about a Christian who said that after twenty years of being a

Christian; he didn't know what he believed anymore after he read a book that cast some aspersions on his Christian faith.

There's a massive atheistic movement going on in the world right now. Tons of movies, especially series, are full of subliminal advertising, and like a malicious flood, they have carried away some Christians as if the believers were paper boats.

To an extent, what we see regularly becomes normal and makes us develop thick skins, even more so in children. When we inundate the world with our narratives, it helps a lot towards the preservation of our offspring and generations to come. The person with the pen wields power and is usually the mightier one. Authors can craft stories anyhow they want, and stories are weapons.

The rainbow is a powerful symbol of God's covenant. It is figurative of God's promises. It loudly reminds us that the storm is over and we will stay afloat and not drown in life's merciless waves. It is a powerful representation of hope. However, unless we strongly own this beautiful sign, it will be hijacked and future generations will be in the dark about its accurate representation.

The cross is not a tool of exorcism; it is a symbol of freedom and love. As physical wood or plastic, it can do zilch to demons and vampires. Its potency lies in getting the revelation of what it truly represents into our hearts. That is when we unleash the force of its power (and it is beyond nuclear).

Life is full of booby traps. But the good news is that akin to Indiana Jones' adventures, we can outwit those traps. How does Indy do it? He overcomes using maps. Let us use our stories to draw maps for the next generation.

Several times, when we come across booby traps as we traverse life's paths, we resort to the map of Jehoshaphat. Charting our course with his map of praise, we safely glide to the other side and ultimately capture the treasure. Without maps, some challenges will shipwreck us.

Writing influences culture strongly. Stronger cultures use stories to subvert weaker ones. Growing up, we always rooted for the cowboy over the Red Indians because the narratives usually had the Red Indians as villains. Hence, with focus and dedication, we can also advance Jesus' Culture through our creativity, love and truth (never through brutal force).

"Until the lion learns how to write, every story will glorify the hunter."— J. Nozipo Maraire.

In the time of Paul, Diana (Artemis) was strongly entrenched in the culture and religion of the Ephesians. That was until Paul came with a different storyline. The story of Jesus subsumed that of Diana and many Ephesians started following Christ. They reconsidered and didn't find their old ways fashionable anymore.

Paul's story triggered winds of change so strong that in a public spectacle, sorcerers made a bonfire of magical books worth bullion vans of dollars.

Diana's image got dented and suffered such a decline in the attention it once commanded that the merchants who sold her memorabilia and artefacts started haemorrhaging money. Enraged, they started a protest and reported Paul to the authorities. That is how powerful a narrative can be.

The person with a stronger narrative wins in the battle of souls. Paul's story is also ours. Before the power of his story toppled systems, he had preached every single day without fail for two years in the hall of Tyrannus.

Take note, unlike modern-day Christians who spend most of the time talking about the "dark" side without proffering solutions, he was not interested in what the worshippers of Diana were doing, he was more focused on his truth.

This is one of the good things that might come out of this COVID season. The church became too insular. We congregated within air-conditioned walls and left many areas of life to become the devil's playground. Turfs like sports, entertainment, and others were abandoned. And he ran amok! This underscores why we must tell our stories. This plot need not remain the same. Let's change it!

Writing is a veritable instrument of war used by kingdoms to rule the souls of men. We have, however, surrendered this force to the dark side to use with impunity as it deems fit. How many Christian movies do we have out there? In this regard, much kudos goes to the Kendrick brothers. And amongst the few, how many are excellent enough to arrest people's attention?

This is where we come in to change the narrative by providing wholesome content for our children and the world.

It is a war!

I wrote earlier that the book of Judges is a book about superheroes. We can create a lot of stories from that book and others to make our children know that intimacy with God can make one a superhero. Samson was a superhero if there ever was any. Like Superman, he also had his kryptonite, which was recklessness and women.

Chapter 4

WHAT DO YOU WRITE ABOUT?

You can write about anything. Don't get locked up in the cage of stereotypes. Christian writing is beyond fiction or nonfiction.

The most important thing is that Christ must be at the bedrock of our writing. He must be the fragrant aroma that fills all in all!

We could write reality shows.

Games are a thing now. We could write games that still kindle adrenaline surges and yet pass on life-changing messages.

WHAT MAKES YOUR PEN A SWORD

1. CREATIVITY

Writing is a creative process. The first thing that the Bible brings to our attention about God is His immense creative ability. Before we got to know about his holiness, mercy, grace, splendour, etc.

In the beginning, God created...

In this light, when He blessed man and said, "Be fruitful, multiply, replenish the world and subdue it," what did he mean? He wants us to be co-creators with him.

CHAPTER 4

Writing is creating something out of nothing and is akin to fashioning radiance out of the darkness. It begins with a spark of inspiration and the rest is history.

Writing is one of the greatest ways we co-create with God.

At the beginning of everything (Genesis), God was creating. At the end of the Bible (Revelation), John was writing.

Creativity also means writing interesting things in masterful ways that enchant. Max Lucado, Mark Batterson, Francine Rivers, Frank Peretti, and several others come to mind here. Max Lucado is an all-time favourite of mine. His poetic prose captivates me every single time.

God caught Moses' attention through unusual ingenuity. A burning tree not consumed was an outlandish spectacle, hence Moses' curiosity was piqued. That must have been quite a sight. The display sucked in the erstwhile Prince of Egypt and made it easy for God to catch, hold his attention, and arm him with a life-transforming message.

There's an interesting point to note here. God did not use his veto power as the Almighty to drag Moses by the scruff of the neck. Instead, He used a colourful bait to reel him in. God was inventively creative.

Will you deliver your message in a jalopy or a sleek Ferrari? The container will always matter. The illustration Jesus made about new wine and new wineskins will never be outdated. New wine doesn't get carried in old, unremarkable wineskins.

Let's all borrow a page from God's book by becoming irresistibly ingenious. The butterfly cannot resist colourful and nectar-filled flowers. The hummingbird cannot resist honeysuckle. Let's create in a way that everybody will find our books, movies, etc., "unputdownable"!

Mediocrity will never cut the mustard. One thing I believe the present global lockdown is telling us is that some of our usual ways of preaching the gospel might go the way of dinosaurs. To learn novel ways requires intense creativity.

How many Christian movies, series, web series, animation and cartoons, musical shows, exist? That's food for thought. If we will fill the earth with the knowledge of God like the waters cover the sea, we must deploy unusual methods.

IMAGINATION

An active imagination is an indispensable writing tool. Like children, we must have flexible and "wild" thoughts.

Children have incredible and elastic imaginations. A child would believe that Superman is real. Thus, it makes sense that we can't access the riches of God's creative kingdom unless we are like kids. The scriptures allude to that.

In my opinion, a mentally inflexible person will struggle to become a wonderful writer, especially in some genres. Frank Peretti was amazing in Piercing the Darkness and This Present Darkness. His books are super-spiritual, but for him to unfurl all those unprecedented thoughts about angels, he engaged astounding imagination.

Remember that at the beginning, before revelation popped up in the form of light, the spirit of God hovered over the black waters. Our imagination must roam wild, wide, and free for us to become remarkable writers. This made people like J. R. R. Tolkien extraordinary. Stretch your mind!

PASSION

Psalms 39:3 KJV My heart was hot within me, while I was musing the fire burned: then spake I with my tongue...

In the above scripture, replace spake and tongue with wrote and fingers. We must burn with passion to become worthy writers. Become a tree that is ablaze and not consumed. It is at this juncture that divinity connects with humanity.

"Light yourself on fire with passion and people will come from miles to watch you burn." John Wesley.

Writing is a marathon and not a sprint. The greatest fuel that can keep you going is passion. If there is no passion, your pen will eventually dry up. Without it, one will run out of gas on the road of purpose.

Over time, I have realized many people are more enthralled with the romantic notions of a subject than the realities surrounding it. Sometimes people approach me for coaching lessons, but when the rubber meets the road, they pull a disappearing act faster than Shazam.

When you exhaust all your literary bullets, passion is that ingredient that keeps you firing still. Paul wrote in prison. John wrote on a barren island. Passion took Christ to the cross and kept Him nailed to its wooden beams.

There were times I almost stopped writing, but the fuel of passion was the only thing that kept me going. There will always be many distractions and times that everything will seem to be a colossal waste of time. At other times, the deserved recognition and rewards refuse to show up. During some periods, you might hit a dry patch and the words refuse to show up. When those seasons show up, passion becomes the battery pack that fires up our creative juices.

PRAYER AND WORSHIP

John was in an atmosphere of prayer and worship when he was told to write.

I am in the prayer unit of my church and a worship team on the side and get most of my inspiration to write during prayer and worship, especially when I speak in tongues. From my experience, speaking in tongues is invaluable to a believer's creativity.

TO THYSELF BE TRUE

Over time, I discovered that I get tremendous flashes of inspiration when I take leisure walks. It makes my spirit and the soil of my mind fertile for the seeds of ideas.

Be in tune with yourself to discover what works for you. We are all wired differently. Some people are more indoorsy than others. Know what floats your creative boat.

BE ENCYCLOPEDIC

O LORD, how great are thy works! And thy thoughts are very deep. Psalms 92:5 KJV

Here, the Psalmist equated the marvellous works of God to the depths of His thoughts. Bottom-line is that mighty works come out of great minds.

To be an outstanding writer, you must be a voracious reader and a great observer of life. Lisa See said, "Read a thousand books, and your words will flow like a river."

Books are to a writing mind what fire is to burning wood. Fueling the mind, they are the uranium to the nuclear power of sublime writing. I dare say you can never be a splendid writer if you don't read copiously and rapaciously. Books also help you know the area/genre you are most inclined towards.

Though the bible has a wide variety of writers, it is noteworthy that erudite people like Moses, Luke, and Paul wrote a good chunk of it.

A few years ago, while on a vacation, I took an early morning walk and stopped by a pond filled with stones. While gazing into it, the stone that David used came to mind and God told me that the ones that He will mostly use in our generation would be well-rounded stones.

The definition of well-rounded is someone skilled, capable, or

CHAPTER 4

knowledgeable about many things (a polymath), or something that covers a lot of different areas or subjects.

To be well-rounded, one must be given to study. Grace will always amplify what it finds available. The oil in the widow's vessel dried up when there were no more vessels. The anointing cannot exist in a vacuum. It runs out when there is no more capacity.

Knowledge is power! For instance, if two writers have the same amount of skill and grace, the one who has more knowledge will most likely be ahead, other things being equal.

Peter and the other apostles saw Jesus in the flesh, but they didn't accomplish what Paul did, especially to the gentiles. Paul was a teacher, philosopher, lawyer, tentmaker, etc.

To become all things to all men takes some prerequisite amount of knowledge. Paul talked sports, wrestling, boxing, and racing amongst other things. In Athens, he debated with the best philosophers of his day, and they could not best him.

One of the best-rounded persons I have met is Pastor Sam Adeyemi, and he is a voracious reader. It is no wonder that he is so amazing!

Francine Rivers is about the best Christian fiction writer of our time. The knowledge and expertise she uses to write her books are wonderful. In the Masterpiece, her research into the art world was profound and colourful. Beyond amazing!

Cindy Trimm is another remarkable minister with prophetic grace. She is an avid reader, a movie buff, and a futurist. While she was ministering at WAFBEC 2020, she mentioned that our future will become like the world in Ready Player One where people lived more online than in the actual world. Her speech motivated me to read the book, and it was great. With the crisis that hit the world, her prophecy is coming true.

At the program, she also said a lot of careers will go extinct as the future unfolds, especially with Artificial Intelligence (AI) gathering steam. However, writing is one skill that will remain evergreen.

Mark Batterson's potent combo of world knowledge and biblical insight make his books delectable offerings. I can't get enough of them.

Knowledge gives writers a sharp edge. Reading other authors will open you up to their thoughts, ideas, and style. One can't but learn. Books are also another magnificent way of getting mentored. Exposure to different things through travelling and keen observation helps a great deal too.

For a Christian writer, the best book of all is the Bible. Like a fish, you must swim in the ocean of this divine book. It is the best resource material ever! Live in it!

Readers are leaders.

GET COACHES AND MENTORS

There is a story that wows me every time. So Moses saw God face to face and beheld the glory of the Father. But surprise, surprise! On their way to the Promised Land, Moses pleaded with Hobab, his brother-in-law, who knew the layout of the wilderness to act as a guide for the children of Israel.

This tells me that we cannot overemphasize the help of someone who knows the terrain you are navigating. Moses had the help of angels, but this time, he needed a human guide and to press it home more; the man was a Midianite. We all must wake up to this reality. We can never dispense with coaches and mentors. Luke was a remarkable writer. However, he had Paul as a mentor.

If you need someone to hold your hand along this journey, resort to https://drekpo.com/

CHAPTER 4

EXCELLENCE

I love seeing stage plays, and the most uninspiring I have seen on a big platform outside the church was a Christian one. It was so flat I almost wept. But I left that day wondering why many people put up a mediocre performance when we tag something, Christian.

It is sad and should stop! God evaluated all his work during creation. He didn't finish any job and take a celestial stroll. He made sure all His works were good before he presented them to man. We should all take a cue from that.

The wonderful people that helped me along my creative journey did so because of the potential of my work and not because of my faith.

Excellence is a journey, though, so at every point in time, we should make sure we are giving our best and working on being the best.

WRITE!!!

Like every other thing, hours and hours of practice are a must-have to become a brilliant writer. Malcolm Gladwell, in his book, Outliers, said that one needs 10,000 hours of practice to become masterful in any area of life.

In The Talent Code, Daniel Coyle makes a substantial case for talent being grown over being natural. He cites example after example to show that continuous practice creates neural pathways that make us exceptional in our vocations.

When I started writing, I was nowhere close to where I am now. I didn't even know how much of a rookie I was until recently; however, I kept at it doggedly.

One Sunday morning, in December 2018, I walked into the church feeling blue because my blog-site hadn't gotten the traction expected. Many questions swam in my head for God's attention.

As I mused, a story I heard somewhere popped into my mind. By this time, praise/worship was going on.

The story had it that God asked a man to push a rock. The dude obeyed and went at it for years, but it was an exercise in futility. One day, out of exhaustion and frustration, he asked God what the big idea was.

God responded that he should inspect himself. He did. By this time, the dude was buffed up with a six-pack, rippling muscles and all. He was in fantastic physical shape.

God told me to check myself out too during that service, and I started smiling. As usual, He had one up on me. My expectations hadn't come through, but I was not the writer I used to be. I had grown in leaps and bounds (still growing).

It took the better part of 10 years for me. We are not all the same, though. A friend reached out to me in December 2018, I think. She wanted some advice and guidance to start a writing career. By the next year, boom! She had written a spectacular book. Boy, she's hot! Our trajectories are also different, just like in every other endeavour in life.

You can never know what you are capable of unless you start. You'll never know how good you are unless you make a move. You'll never know your weaknesses and strengths unless you step out of your comfort zone. Whatever the surrounding limitations might be, just start!

Our Lord is a God of process.

Through my blogging, I developed a network and met others who assisted me on the journey. The two people that have encouraged and assisted me the most are not Christians. But they found my work appealing and offered me all the help I needed. Amazing people!

When we step out in courage and determination, things align. The wise men showed up when Jesus was born, even though he was in a nondescript manger.

The Yoruba people have a saying that it's the child that raises his or her arms that adults lift to the skies. It is when the student is ready that the teacher appears. The teacher can only pay attention when your effort is visible. No one wants to spend energy and time on a fruitless venture.

You can start by posting articles on your social media spaces. You

CHAPTER 4

can start a blog. I have a Facebook group for Christian writers called Christian Writers' and Authors' Network (CWAN). There is another called Heaven'z Beatz where we write about inspirational songs. We put up posts to encourage and inspire one another. You can become a part of these movements.

Dare to start and you'll see that the horizons are unending.

If this is a journey that you strongly believe in, following this course, you can check out my online course and writing coach services on https://drekpo.com/

With these basics, I believe, I have been able to nudge you on to this great, fulfilling and purposeful path of writing for Christ.

In another book, we will explore some of these points further. Meanwhile, type away and allow your keyboard no rest.

Thank you once again for the privilege of reading. The honour is mine.

You can follow me on
Podcast: https://anchor.fm/ekpo-eze
Blog-site https://drekpo.com/
Twitter: @docekpo
Instagram: The Doctor Scribe @docekpo
Facebook Group: Christian Writers' and Authors' Network (CWAN)
Facebook Group: Heavenz Muzik

I look forward to your reviews, especially on Amazon. You can send questions and inquiries to ekpoeze@gmail.com

Conclusion

God speaks and changes our lives through the greatest stories ever! To change the world, we must do the same.

Kindly leave your reviews.

Thank you.

Dr Ekpo Ezechinyere.

Epilogue

Write the things which thou hast seen, and the things which are, and the things which shall be hereafter... Revelation 1:19

Afterword

The only way to counter a destructive narrative is by fashioning a creative one.

And the earth was without form, and void; and darkness was upon the face of the deep. And the Spirit of God moved upon the face of the waters. And God said, Let there be light: and there was light.
   Genesis 1:2-3

About the Author

Dr Ekpo Ezechinyere is a medical doctor, who graduated from the University of Ibadan. After practising for many years, he became the Chief Operating Officer (COO) of one of the Health Maintenance Organisations (HMO) in Nigeria.

These days, Dr Ezechinyere empowers people, mostly younger folks, to live inspired through his blog-site www.drekpo.com and other social media platforms.

Using the instrumentality of stories and creative writing, he brings the bible into high definition reality by emulating how Jesus used parables to drive home enduring truths.

A creative consultant, trainer and coach, he consulted for www.theiibc.com and managed their inspirational series.

Dr Ekpo co-wrote Strain (www.strainthemovie.com) which recently won the Urban Film Festival, Best International Movie of 2020 in Miami, Florida. The movie was also nominated by the Toronto International Nollywood Film Festival 2020 for Best Nollywood Drama, Best African Film, and Best International Film. The Festival International De Cinema De Kinshasa gave it a nomination too.

He has learnt a lot all these years, is still voraciously learning and has several other books in the pipeline. Ernest Hemingway said, "We are all apprentices in a craft where no one ever becomes a master."

Dr Ekpo is a coach, trainer, bookworm, an avid follower of Football and WWE, a video game buff, a foodie, an amala enthusiast, a Marvel and DC devotee, and he lives continually in an ocean of inspiring music.

Crazy Fact: His dream as a young boy was to become a WWE wrestler.

He is married to Dr Lilian Ekpo and has two sons, Othniel-Ryan and Zane-Jordan.

You can connect with me on:
- https://drekpo.com
- https://twitter.com/docekpo
- https://www.facebook.com/eezechinyere

Subscribe to my newsletter:
- http://bit.ly/CWANOCT_1

Also by DR EKPO EZECHINYERE

Printed in Great Britain
by Amazon